Heirs to Ambedkar

Heirs to Ambedkar

THE REBIRTH OF ENGAGED BUDDHISM IN INDIA

Alan Senauke

Clear View Press • Berkeley

Published by Clear View Press
1933 Russell Street
Berkeley, CA 94703
www.clearviewproject.org

Library of Congress Cataloguing-in-Publication Data
Senauke, Alan.
Heirs To Ambedkar: The Rebirth of Engaged Buddhism in India
ISBN: 9780-982784426
1. Engaged Buddhism. 2. Zen Buddhism. 3. Human Rights—Asia.
4. Race & Civil Rights—India.

Edition 2, January 2015

Cover photograph by Alan Senauke.

ISBN: 0982784422
ISBN 13: 9780982784426

With justice on our side, I do not see how we can lose our battle. The battle to me is a matter of joy... For ours is a battle not for wealth or for power. It is a battle for freedom. It is a battle for the reclamation of the human personality.

— Dr. B. R. Ambedkar,
All-India Depressed Classes Conference, 1942

Introduction

I FIRST HEARD ABOUT DR. Ambedkar, about the conversion of India's Untouchables to Buddhism, and a new Buddhist movement in India, from reading *Jai Bhim—Dispatches from a Peaceful Revolution*, by Terry Pilchik (Nagabodhi). At the time, around the year 1989, I was working for *Jai Bhim's* publisher Parallax Press, which continues today to issue books by Thich Nhat Hanh and other engaged Buddhist writers. I met Dhammachari Nagabodhi, a senior member of what was then Friends of the Western Buddhist Order (FWBO), while he traveled in the U.S. to support his book. What I read and heard from him personally was compelling. There were fifty million practicing Buddhists in India, coming to liberation from an environment of discrimination and poverty, and the wider world knew almost nothing about them or their movement. I wanted to see this for myself.

A year or two later I began working as director of the Buddhist Peace Fellowship. At BPF we were linked with engaged Buddhists across the United States and throughout Asia. Among our Asian connections was the International Network of Engaged Buddhists (INEB), headquartered in Thailand and founded by the Thai Buddhist activist, writer, and philosopher Sulak Sivaraksa. Ajahn Sulak and his staff made an effort to include Ambedkarite Buddhists in the periodic INEB conferences. But initially the Ambedkarite representatives were less spiritual or religious, and more on the political side of things, often advocating militant and confrontational strategies surprising to a gathering of non-violent Buddhist activists.

In time, INEB connected with leading members of FWBO and its Indian wing, Triratna Bauddha Mahāsangha (TBM). Via INEB I became friends with Mangesh Dahiwale and Dhammachari Maitreyanath, two TBM leaders who were visiting Buddhist communities and groups like BPF in the U.S., lecturing about Ambedkar and India's Dalits, and building support for their Buddhist movement. These new friends invited me to visit India and learn firsthand about their community work. It took more than a year to make the right arrangements, but that first trip to India opened my eyes. I have been going regularly ever since.

The main purpose of going to India, at least the first time, was to bear witness—to open myself to the complexity, crowds, and messiness of India, all the things we in the West might understandably consider overwhelming. But I also knew my Buddhist friends—I never felt alone—and I trusted that I was going to see and be in a community. That has always been the case.

Returning to this community each year, there is still much for me to see and learn. I feel that I am always scratching the surface of Indian life. It has been possible, however, to see how good friends can be of service. We can teach, we can organize funds and resources, we can tell others back in the West and even in other sectors of Indian society what we have seen in cities like Mumbai, Nagpur, and Pune that leaves us hopeful about the future of Buddha's way. In other words, we can use our privilege to help people raise themselves to be bodhisattvas, to help others find freedom.

That is the purpose of this little book: to encourage, to inspire, and to see ourselves walking side by side with peoples we never knew were there. May all beings be happy. May all beings have a wide, clear view of our interdependent life.

Engaged Buddhism

*Positively, my social philosophy may be said to be en-
shrined in three words: liberty, equality and fraternity.
Let no one however say that I have borrowed my philosophy from the French Revolution. I have not. My
philosophy has its roots in religion and not in political
science. I have derived them from the teachings of my
master, the Buddha.*

— Dr. B. R. Ambedkar, BBC
Radio address, 1942

ARRIVING IN INDIA AT MIDNIGHT after endless hours in
flight, leaving the Mumbai airport, looking out the taxi
window at bustling streets—first impressions stay with
me. There was the late-night hum of a great city winding
down. Pot-holed thoroughfares. Glittering apartment
towers encircled by garbage-strewn lots. Ragged-clothed

men, women, and families huddled in sleep by the side of the road. Words spoken quickly and with an edge of energy.

I have been elsewhere in South Asia—Burma, Bangladesh, and Sri Lanka—where war and civil strife prevail. But in India I sense a freedom and intimacy in the streets, despite the jarring discrepancies of wealth and standing. There is something about the fact that India is the world's largest democracy. Indian democracy is wild, corrupt, and every bit as flawed as what we call American democracy. Still the energy of India's people is limitless. It all feels strangely familiar to me, or familial in the best (and maybe in the worst) sense of the word.

India is the birthplace of Shakyamuni Buddha, the taproot of the Buddhist practice I have followed for more than thirty years. So, in a way, I was returning to the source. Buddhism was the dominant religious and cultural force in India for over fifteen hundred years, from the Buddha's birth in the sixth century BCE until the Muslim conquest of India in the thirteenth century. Seven hundred fifty years later, in the middle of the twentieth century, Buddhism was reborn in India among Dalit or "ex-Untouchable" communities I have come to know and love.

This new Indian Buddhism—as it has emerged in the last sixty years among India's Untouchable and tribal peoples, those who have been discarded by society—is what some people call "engaged Buddhism." My own thinking about engaged Buddhism is well-expressed by the Vietnamese Zen Master Thich Nhat Hanh:

> Engaged Buddhism is just Buddhism. When bombs begin to fall on people, you cannot stay in the meditation hall all of the time. Meditation is about the awareness of what is going on—not only in your body and in your feelings, but all around you.

India's modern Buddhist movement, as you will see, arises in the midst of an ancient ongoing struggle. Not a war with the bright flash and crash of bombs, but systematic oppression, exploitation, and a quiet kind of violence, the violence of caste, where one sector of society is forever under the thumb of another. This struggle was seen by visionary Indian leaders, names unknown to us in the West—but most prominently B. R. Ambedkar, who led an Indian movement for human rights and for the deconstruction of India's brutal caste system, from the 1920s until his death in 1956. (In telling ways, Ambedkar's movement paralleled, intertwined, and contrasted with the anti-colonial movement led by Gandhi and Nehru.) By the 1950s Dr. Ambedkar came to believe that the teachings and values of the Buddhist tradition, born in India twenty-five hundred years earlier, offered a foundation for the successful, nonviolent transformation of Indian society. I think of this as engaged Buddhism.

From very early times, as Brahmanic or Vedic culture took shape in India, there arose four traditional *varnas* or caste delineations, a hierarchical system that defined and limited the scope of social interactions (about which more later). *Varna* is a Sanskrit word meaning "color," suggesting that early caste distinctions were based on perception of skin color. *Brahmin* is the highest or Hindu priestly caste. Historically the *Kshatriyas* make up the warrior caste. The *Vaishyas* include farmers, merchants, and artisans. *Shudras* are servants and manual laborers. The broad occupational distinctions were and are often overlooked, but the three highest castes were considered noble or *arya,* participating in Vedic rituals, which are proscribed for *Shudras. Untouchables* occupy a social position that is outside of and beneath even the lowest of castes. Seen as less than human, their traditional occupations include tasks considered by caste Hindus as inherently polluting or degrading.

The Buddha himself, a prince of the Sakya clan in northern India, was born into the Kshatriya caste. Coming to enlightenment after years of meditation, he had a radical social vision. He created a fourfold *sangha* or community of monks, nuns, laymen, and laywomen. At a time when caste was solidifying into a rigid hereditary system he admitted men and women from every background into his order, and affirmed their capacity for enlightenment. Joining the Buddha's community was a way for people of every stratum to reframe their social identity.

> Just as, O monks, the great rivers Ganga, Yamuna, Aciravati, Sarabhu, and Mahi, on reaching the ocean, lose their earlier name and identity and come to be reckoned as the great ocean, similarly, O monks, people of the four castes (*varnas*).... who leave the household and become homeless recluses under the Doctrine and Discipline declared by the Tathagata, lose their previous names and identities and are reckoned as recluses who are sons of Sakya.

As the Buddha explains in an early *sutta*, admission to the sangha was based on how one lived, not where one was born.

> Birth makes not a man an outcast,
> Birth makes not a man a brahmin;
> Action makes a man an outcast,
> Action makes a man a brahmin.

The modern term "engaged Buddhism" or "socially engaged Buddhism" was coined by Thich Nhat Hanh, merging his active experience of Vietnamese Buddhism and his study of French existentialism, which emerged from a crucible of the Second World War upholding a principle of *engagement*. Jean Paul Sartre and other French intellectuals saw *engagement* as "the process of accepting responsibility for the political consequences of one's actions." When Thich Nhat Hanh asserts, "Engaged Buddhism is just Buddhism," he is speaking to an understanding of the Buddha's original way. The Buddha and his sangha lived in the midst of society. They didn't set up their monasteries and *viharas* on isolated mountaintops. They depended on laywomen and men, *upasika* and *upasaka*, for the requisites of life—food, clothing, shelter, and medicine. Even today, monks and nuns in Southeast Asia go out into the towns and villages where they live on alms rounds for food each morning. Although monks and nuns have always maintained a strict monastic discipline, it is mistaken to imagine that monasteries are cloistered and apart from brothers and sisters in the secular world. All of human society is mutually dependent.

Engaged Buddhism has to do with a willingness to turn towards suffering, our own suffering and that of other people; to understand how we have fashioned whole systems of suffering out of caste, race, class, and gender; and to know that, interdependently and individually, all of us co-create this suffering.

In terms of the Buddha's teaching, the practice of awakening flows from an understanding of basic principles that Buddha discovered and expounded. The Four Noble Truths teach about suffering, the cause of suffering, that there can be an end to suffering, and that there is a path or a way to live life to arrive at the end of suffering. The Buddha's discovery of dependent co-arising (*paticcasamuppada*) explains that all that we see and experience in the world arises from previous causes and conditions, and that our actions create the causes for future conditions. The *Assutava Sutta* puts this complex principle into simple language:

> When this is, that is.
> From the arising of this
> comes the arising of that.
> When this isn't, that isn't.
> From the cessation of this comes
> the cessation of that.

The Mahayana tradition, an early development of Indian Buddhism, upholds the Bodhisattva vow as a first principle: the personal vow to save all sentient beings— including oneself—from suffering. As Dr. Ambedkar came to see, our liberation and the liberation of others are inseparable.

Ambedkar and the Hell of Caste

There is no doubt, in my opinion, that unless you change your social order you can achieve little by way of progress...You cannot build anything on the foundations of caste. You cannot build up a nation, you cannot build up a morality. Anything you will build on the foundations of caste will crack and will never be a whole.

— Dr. B. R. Ambedkar: *Annihilation of Caste*, 1936

MY BUDDHIST FRIENDS GREET EACH other with a warm salutation: "Jai Bhim!" This means "Victory to Bhim," Dr. Bhimrao Ambedkar, the visionary twentieth-century leader of India's Buddhists.

Today, a Buddhist revolution is taking place in the land of Shakyamuni, a revolution hidden in plain sight. These Indian Buddhists, the Untouchable castes and tribal peoples, among the poorest of the poor, go by various names: neo-Buddhists, Dalit Buddhists, Navayanists, Ambedkarites. Like so much in the lives of these people, these various names carry an odor of discrimination—that theirs is something other than real Buddhism. To my mind, the opposite is true. The Buddhism that Ambedkar brought to his own Untouchable communities is precisely the practice of Buddha, Dharma, Sangha or, as Ambedkar put it, of Liberty, Equality, and Fraternity. Buddhism is the expression of liberated beings, the kernel of a liberated and casteless society. Today it is alive among millions in India, and this may well become the largest community of Buddhist practitioners on the planet.

Bhimrao Ramji Ambedkar (or Babasaheb, as his devotees call him) was born in 1891 to a poor but educated Mahar family. Traditionally the Mahars—the largest Untouchable caste in the region of Maharashtra—lived outside the boundaries of a village and worked as servants, watchmen, street-sweepers, and haulers of animal carcasses. Dr. Ambedkar's father, Ramji Sakpal, served in the colonial Indian army, where he was schooled in Marathi and English. He instilled a love of learning in his children and lobbied for their admission to government schools. But Untouchable students often had to hear their lessons while crouched outside the classroom window. By virtue of his brilliance and good fortune the young Ambedkar was among the first Untouchables to attend an Indian university, gaining a degree in economics and political science from the prestigious Bombay University. With scholarship support from the Gayakwad ruler of Baroda state, Ambedkar went on to earn doctorates from Columbia University and the London School of Economics, and a place at the bar at London's Gray's Inn by his early thirties. He came back from the West as one of the best-educated men in India. But returning from England to work as a finance secretary for his benefactor, the Gayakwad of Baroda, he was unable to find housing, and was barred from dining with his colleagues. He suffered the indignity of his own clerks tossing files on his desk for fear of his "polluting" touch.

The "hell of caste" that Ambedkar experienced in his youth is hard for many of us in the West to imagine, despite our own history of slavery, race, and the twentieth-century civil rights movement. Indian caste still means hereditary bondage passed from generation to generation under a dominant Brahmanic or Hindu social system. Contrary to the Buddhist meaning of these same words, in this system *karma* means fate or the caste one is born into, and *dharma* means the duty to live out one's life within the confines of caste proscriptions and expectations. Even today this duty includes strict endogamy, or marriage only within one's caste, ensuring a fixed heredity. In daily life, untouchability precludes those of different castes, or non-castes, from living within the bounds of a village, sharing food or drink, having access to education, or entering Hindu temples. Seen as "unclean," even the shadow of an Untouchable is considered polluting to caste Hindus. These forms of discrimination can be found in many parts of India, most strongly in rural areas.

Although he never used the term, "Dalit" is another commonly heard name for the Untouchable community Dr. Ambedkar was born into. Among Dr. Ambedkar's followers, some use "Dalit" as a convenience and others find it demeaning. It means people who are "broken to pieces" or suppressed. It contrasts with Ambedkar's Indian contemporary Gandhi's term for Untouchables—*harijan,* which means "children of god." Given that Untouchables felt themselves to be neither children nor under divine provenance, *harijan* never found wide acceptance among them. Other names have been suggested, each problematic, seen as demeaning by one group or another. Under British colonial rule they were known as Depressed Classes. In the Indian constitution they are listed as Scheduled Classes and Scheduled Tribes, with an ever-changing roster of several thousand designated population groups. The word "Untouchable" is a legally proscribed status; "ex-Untouchable" is euphemism.

Dalits or Untouchables find themselves beneath even the lowest rungs of the caste system ladder, which would be the Shudras and low caste groups known as Other Backward Classes (or OBC) who experience similar social, economic, and educational discrimination. Dalits, OBC, and tribal people together comprise more than sixty percent of India's 1.27 billion people (2013 estimate).

The 2001 census puts India's Buddhist population at eight million, more than ninety percent from Dalit communities. (Scholars suggest the numbers of uncounted or undeclared Buddhists are more likely in the range of thirty million.) These communities are distributed across the nation—as is the overall Dalit population of more than 200 million—with the largest concentration of Buddhists in the Indian state of Maharashtra. Buddhist identity is rooted in Indian history, but it was reclaimed by Ambedkar just sixty years ago, entwined with his assertion of political and social freedom.

The many Untouchable or Dalit communities, differentiated by region, ethnicity, and subcaste, have been identified with occupations such as butchering, removal of rubbish, sweeping, removal of human waste and dead animals, leatherwork, and so on. Jobs like this are still seen as impure activities, polluting to higher castes, and somehow contagious. Viewed as impure, Untouchables were systematically excluded from aspects of ordinary Hindu life.

Human Rights Watch reports:

> India's Untouchables are relegated to the lowest jobs, and live in constant fear of being publicly humiliated, paraded naked, beaten, and raped with impunity by upper-caste Hindus seeking to keep them in their place. Merely walking through an upper-caste neighborhood is a life-threatening offense.

A 2010 study compiled by the World Council of Churches, the World Student Christian Federation, and the World YWCA says:

> Recent statistics indicate that every week in Dalit communities across India there are:
> - 13 murders
> - 5 Dalit homes burnt
> - 6 Dalit people kidnapped or abducted
> - 21 Dalit women raped

Atrocities against Dalit people are a daily occurrence. The Scheduled caste and scheduled Tribes (Prevention of Atrocities) Act 1989 in India defines the type of abuses, which are illegal, including:

- forcing Dalit people to eat obnoxious substances
- assaulting Dalit women with intent to dishonor and outrage their modesty
- using a position of dominance to sexually exploit a Dalit woman
- corrupting or fouling a Dalit water source

By listing these and other offences, the law reveals the awareness of the many ways in which Dalit and Tribal people are subject to indignity, violence and abuse. It is estimated that a crime is committed against a Dalit person every 18 minutes. The problem for many is not the law but the lack of political will, at local and national levels, to apply it. In 2006, the official conviction rate for Dalit atrocity cases was just 5.3%. The statistics are horrifying:

- In rural areas, 37.8% of government run schools make Dalit children sit separately from other children
- In 27.6% of rural villages, Dalits are prevented from entering police stations
- In 33% of rural villages, public health workers refuse to enter Dalit homes
- 48.4% of Dalit villages are denied access to water sources
- In 70% of rural villages, Dalit and non-Dalit people cannot eat together.

Untouchability was legally abolished by India's secular constitution of 1950, bolstered by continuing protective legislation. But the real conditions of Dalit life are not much improved today. Juliette de Rivera of Human Rights Watch writes, "New laws are useless unless they are implemented, as we have seen with previous efforts to ensure protection of Dalit rights." This is particularly true in rural India, where legal process and cosmopolitan views are hard to come by. In a June 2003 edition of *National Geographic News* Hillary Maxwell wrote:

> Human rights abuses against these people, known as Dalits, are legion. A random sampling of headlines in mainstream Indian newspapers tells their story: "Dalit boy beaten to death for plucking flowers;" "Dalit tortured by cops for three days;" "Dalit 'witch' paraded naked in Bihar;" "Dalit killed in lock-up at Kurnool;" "Seven Dalits burnt alive in caste clash;" "Five Dalits lynched in Haryana;" "Dalit woman gang-raped, paraded naked;" "Police egged on mob to lynch Dalits."

Maxwell adds:

> India's Untouchables are relegated to the lowest jobs, and live in constant fear of being publicly humiliated, paraded naked, beaten, and raped with impunity by upper-caste Hindus seeking

to keep them in their place. Merely walking through an upper-caste neighborhood is a life-threatening offense.

Dalit women have to reckon with a threefold oppression: caste, poverty, and gender discrimination, even within their own communities. Rape and sexual violence are India's shame, cutting across all caste and economic lines.

In a 2013 report, Rashida Manjoo, the UN Special Rapporteur on violence against women, singled out the oppression of Dalit women:

> Many experience some of the worst forms of discrimination. The reality of Dalit women and girls is one of exclusion and marginalization, which perpetuates their subordinate position in society and increases their vulnerability, throughout generations.

These are the harsh realities Dr. Ambedkar faced in the 1920s and '30s. Between 1923 and the 1950s he worked in the political system as a tireless advocate for rights of all Indians. While Gandhi was forging a nonviolent anti-colonial movement, Ambedkar—who often clashed with Gandhi—worked for human rights and the annihilation of caste, in contrast to what many saw as an otherwise elite-driven nationalism. After years of attempted collaboration with reformist Hindus, including Gandhi and Nehru, Ambedkar, a member of the Bombay legislature and a leader of the Mahar conference, organized a 1927 nonviolent *satyagraha* (meaning, roughly, "truthforce") of thousands to draw water and drink from the Chowdar Tank, a reservoir closed to Untouchables despite a 1923 resolution of the Bombay Council. Later that year, Ambedkar took the radical symbolic step of publicly burning the *Manusmrti,* the revered Brahmanic code of caste duty, which he and other leaders saw as key to the social, economic, religious, and political oppression of the Untouchables.

By 1935 Dr. Ambedkar concluded that the dominant Brahmin/Hindu caste system could not be reformed even with support from most liberal-minded Hindus. He argued that caste oppression was not an artifact of Brahmanism, but its essence. Ambedkar urged the Untouchables to give up the idea of attaining Hindu religious rights. He saw caste as a "system of graded inequality," in which each subcaste measures itself above some castes and below others, creating an almost infinite factionalism, dividing each exploited community against another, making unity of social or political purpose almost impossible. He prepared to leave Hinduism and adopt another religion. Ambedkar said: "I was born a Hindu, but I solemnly assure you that I will not die as a Hindu." For fifteen years he investigated Islam, Christianity, and Sikhism—and was courted by each of these groups, who were well aware that Ambedkar's conversion would bring along millions of Untouchables and the promise of wide political power.

Ambedkar had decided by the early 1940s that Buddhism—indigenous to India, where it had been the defining religious tradition for nearly fifteen hundred years—was the logical home for his people. He wrote:

> The teachings of Buddha are eternal, but even then Buddha did not proclaim them to be infallible. The religion of Buddha has the capacity to change according to times, a quality which no other religion can claim to have...Now what is the basis of Buddhism? If you study carefully, you will see that Buddhism is based on reason. There is an element of flexibility inherent in it, which is not found in any other religion.

But plans for conversion were postponed while, at the invitation of India's first prime minister Jawaharal Nehru, Dr. Ambedkar served as law minister and leader of the constitutional drafting committee. His work on the constitution bore fruit in a remarkable document that establishes in law the very principles of freedom and justice that Ambedkar had preached for decades.

In the early 1950s, setting aside his political career, he plunged into the study of Buddhism and its application to the shaping of a new identity for many millions.

In the spring of 1950 he wrote a radical and influential article, "Buddha and the Future of His Religion," which was published in *Maha Bodhi*, the widely read English-language journal of the Indian Maha Bodhi Society.

> (The Buddha) told Ananda that His religion was based on reason and experience and that his followers should not accept his teaching as correct and binding merely because they emanated from Him. Being based on reason and experience they were free to modify or even to abandon any of his teachings if it was found that at a given time and in given circumstances they do not apply. He wished His religion not to be encumbered with the dead wood of the past. He wanted that it should remain evergreen and serviceable at all times.

After long consideration and consultation, and in ill health, feeling the shadow of mortality, Dr. Ambedkar converted on October 14, 1956 at the Deekshabhoomi (Conversion Ground) in Nagpur, taking the Three Refuges in Buddha, Dharma, and Sangha, and receiving the *pancasila,* or five ethical precepts, from the senior Buddhist monk in India, U Chandramani. Then he did an unprecedented thing, particularly unprecedented for a layperson. Turning to four hundred thousand

Untouchable followers who were present, he offered them the refuges and his own twenty-two vows, which included the five precepts and the renunciation of specific articles of Hindu practice and belief.

The following day Ambedkar explained why he chose Nagpur as the locus of conversion.

> Many people ask me why Nagpur was decided upon for this work...Those who read Buddhist history will come to know that in India, if anyone spread Buddhism, it was the Nag people. The Nag people were fearful enemies of the Aryans. A Fierce and fighting war went on between the Aryans and non-Aryans. Examples of the harassment of the Nags by the Aryan people are found in the Puranas...Those Nag people who endured so much suffering wanted some great man to raise them up. They met that great man in Gautam Buddha. The Nag people spread the teaching of Bagwan Buddha all over India. Thus we are like Nag people. It seems that the Nag people lived chiefly in Nagpur and the surrounding country. So they call this city Nagpur, meaning city of Nags. About 27 miles from here the Nag Nadi River flows. Of course the name of the river comes from the people living here.

This act of conscious conversion signaled a momentous renewal of Buddhism in India. A number of mass conversions followed within weeks. But by early December, less than two months later, Dr. Ambedkar had died from complications of diabetes and heart disease.

Sixty-five years later, in Mumbai's Bandra East slums, in Pune's Dapodi neighborhood, in the children's hostels and schools of Nagpur, one sees modest storefront or roadside *viharas*—with a Buddha and an image of Dr. Ambedkar, each adorned with garlands of fresh flowers—where people sing the Pali chants, sit in meditation, and hear the dharma. The Buddha's message is still clear. He said: "I teach about suffering and the end of suffering." For those who suffer from poverty and discrimination day by day and year by year, this message is hope itself. They see a rare opportunity to create for themselves a new identity. With the enduring leadership of Dr. Ambedkar, many thousands have taken to Buddhism because they can and because they must.

The New Buddhist Movement

It would be difficult to find a religious teacher to compare with Buddha, whose teachings embrace so many aspects of the social life of people, whose doctrines are so modern and with main concern to give salvation to man in his life on earth and not to promise it in heaven after he is dead!

— Dr. B. R. Ambedkar,
from *Buddha and the Future of His Religion*, 1950

DESPITE THE BUDDHIST CONVERSION MOVEMENT of millions, Dr. Ambedkar's death left the spiritual and political movement of Untouchables unfinished and without leadership. Given the entrenched influence of caste and subcaste, it was not surprising to see the rapid rise of political and organizational factionalism among the Dalits. The Ambedkarite movement itself was divided, with some taking up what we now call identity-politics and militancy—a militancy that does not always cleave to nonviolent principles, some turning towards Buddhism as religion, and some finding a blend of both. No one remaining on the scene had Ambedkar's intellectual gifts and strength of character with which to unify the many outcast communities into one movement.

Mangesh Dahiwale of the Manuski Center says:

> People looked at Dr. Babasaheb Ambedkar as a kind of guide or guru or philosopher who would lead them after conversion. *The Buddha and His Dhamma* was published a year after Dr. Ambedkar's death and it became a source that people turned towards to understand Buddhism. It was published in English first, and then soon translated in Marathi and Hindi. That book was a guide, and people began to read it and study it in study groups.

There were few Buddhist teachers in India during and after Ambedkar's time. But small groups of Theravada monks traveled across India. As Mangesh explains:

> Naturally people flocked around the Sri Lankan and Burmese Buddhists, anyone who could offer Buddhist teachings. If they found a bhikkhu, they

would gather around and try to understand what Buddhism is. In fact some from the Ambedkarite movement in the 1950s became monks in India, ordained in the Sri Lankan tradition.

Dr. Ambedkar had hoped, maybe even had assumed, that the Indian conversion movement would be a beacon to monks and teachers from all the Buddhist nations of Asia. Ambedkar wrote optimistically in his 1950 essay, "Buddha and the Future of His Religion":

If the new world—which be it realised is very different from the old—must have a religion—and the new world needs religion far more than the old world did—then it can only be religion of the Buddha.

But this was not to be...at least not yet. The painful fact is that Buddhists in Asian and Western dharma communities paid scant attention to the rebirth of Buddhism in India. Like the oppression of caste, the needs and realities of the most oppressed have been almost invisible to those privileged to live outside the Indian circle of caste oppression. The process Dr. Ambedkar set in motion was incomplete. From 1956 until the early 1980s there was little continuing education or practice available to millions who had converted in the initial movement. Although he had begun building connections with other Buddhist cultures, Ambedkar was critical of institutional Buddhism in India and elsewhere in Asia. He was particularly critical of the contemporary monks' sangha, which he criticized as elitist and, to a degree, self-serving.

> The Bhikkhu Sangha in its present condition can therefore be of no use for the spread of Buddhism...There is in them neither learning nor service...We want fewer Bhikkhus and we want Bhikkhus highly educated...The Bhikkhus of today must return to the old ideal.

Dr. Ambedkar had a powerful social interpretation of the Buddha's teachings, which empowered the poor and the oppressed—much as Liberation Theology has served the Catholic oppressed in Latin America. Ambedkar understood the Buddha's acceptance of men and women of every background and caste into his community to be a radical social statement that undermined the stratified society of his times.

> A people and their religion must be judged by social standards based on social ethics. No other standard would have any meaning if religion is held to be necessary good for the well-being of the people.

Daring to offer refuge and precepts to many thousands immediately after taking refuge himself—this was a bold step that offended status-conscious monks. His death just weeks later left little time to water the dharma seeds. But the right seeds had been planted. According to Mangesh Dahiwale:

> Babasaheb Ambedkar had created the Bhartiya Bauddha Mahasabha or the Buddhist Society of India in 1955. The first mass conversions were held under their auspices. But for the most part these were local initiatives, because people were acting locally. The start of this movement was grassroots and Indian led. Really there were no teachers or prominent leaders, because ordinary people took the initiative. Even though Dr. Ambedkar was not there, his inspiration was there. People tried to do what they could. Mainly they were very poor, facing discrimination, but they tried to keep the flame alive.

The network of local *viharas* and practitioners created by Ambedkar and by the conversion movement scattered across Maharastra and other parts of India, allowed a young English monk, Ven. Sangharakshita, to connect with the Dalit Buddhists. From earlier years in India Sangharakshita, who likewise had a social understanding of the Buddha's teachings, was strongly called to work with these new Indian Buddhists. Before Ambedkar's death they had an opportunity to meet several times. By chance, Sangharakshita had been in Nagpur the evening Ambedkar passed away in Delhi, and was asked to speak at a meeting of condolence. He writes:

> By the time I rose to speak—standing on the seat of a rickshaw, and with someone holding a microphone in front of me—about 100,000 people had gathered. By rights I should have been the last speaker but as things turned out I was the first. In fact I was the only speaker. Not that there were not others who wanted to pay tribute to the memory of the departed leader. One by one, some five or six of Ambedkar's most prominent local supporters attempted to speak, and one by one they were forced to sit down again as, overcome by emotion, they burst into tears after uttering only a few words.

From this moment Sangharakshita's sense of personal responsibility was clear.

> During the decade that followed I spent much of my time with the ex-Untouchable Buddhists of Nagpur, Bombay, Poona, Jabalpur, and

Ahmedabad, as well as with those who lived in the small towns and villages of central and western India. I learned to admire their cheerfulness, their friendliness, their intelligence, and their loyalty to the memory of their great emancipator.

Returning to Great Britain, where he founded the Friends of the Western Buddhist Order (FWBO), Sangharakshita never forgot about the Dalit Buddhists and his friends in India. He encouraged a young disciple, Lokamitra, to visit India and think about working with the Ambedkarite Buddhists.

Dhammachari Lokamitra is a tall, solid, and youthful-looking Englishman with an easy laugh and a quick mind. His energy at sixty-five hints at a kind of wildness tempered by years of dharma practice. Lokamitra lives with his family in a modest house in the Ambedkar Colony settlement of Pune. Since 1978 he has helped to build a wide-ranging organization which is now called Triratna Bauddha Mahasangha/ TBM, the Indian wing of the Triratna Buddhist Community (formerly the Friends of the Western Buddhist Order/FWBO), the most extensive network of Buddhist practice and training centers in India. TBM is linked with a variety of related social organizations, all which are aimed at developing a new Indian or Ambedkarite Buddhism, fusing dharma practice and social action.

TBM's literature offers this self-description:

> The Triratna Bauddha Mahasangha has meditation and Dhamma study centers in many Indian states, and has been in contact with hundreds of thousands of people through retreats, classes and public programmes. The movement is guided by ordained members of the Triratna Bauddha Sangha.
>
> The essence of Buddhism is timeless and universal, but the forms it takes always adapt according to context. The Triratna Bauddha Mahasangha

is dedicated to communicating Buddhist truths in ways appropriate to the modern world.

Lokamitra first came to India in 1977 to study yoga in Pune with B. S. Iyengar. Breaking the long train trip from Calcutta in Nagpur, he happened to arrive on the twenty-first anniversary of Dr. Ambedkar's conversion. As an FWBO *angarika,* wearing robes, he was respectfully given a place on a large stage at the Deekshabhoomi, facing thousands of Ambedkar's devotees.

> In the 36 hours we spent in Nagpur I entered a new world, a world of millions of the most oppressed people, all desperate to transform their lives and their society through Buddhism, but with little living teaching to guide them. I had stumbled blindly into a situation in which the twofold transformation seemed a real possibility, and on the most auspicious of days. I did not consciously decide to live and work in India then but I have no doubt that my future was decided on that day.

Lokamitra moved to India the following year. With help of local Buddhist friends, he organized retreats and meditation groups. He says, "Our friends organized these where they could, a disused railway carriage, the veranda of an unfinished police station, a small garage when its car went to church on Sundays."

More than thirty years have passed since those rough and ready days. TBM now includes five hundred Indian order members and many thousands of practitioners. With the support of Karuna Trust in Great Britain and other donors in Asia and the West, two related organizations have evolved—Bahujan Hitay (meaning "for the welfare of many") and Jambudvipa Trust—to do outreach and social work among the Dalits. More recently they have created the Manuski Project—where I stay when I am in Pune. Pune—the ninth largest urban center in India, only seventy-five miles from Mumbai on the edge of the Deccan Plateau—is a focal point for Dalit community and social work. The Manuski center building, just behind a new highway, is quiet and cool, with a good library, meeting rooms, offices, a number of basic but comfortable guest rooms, and a large meditation hall. Manuski is the Marathi word Dr. Ambedkar used for "humanity" or "humanness." The center's mission is:

1. Transcending caste barriers through Social Development Programs
2. Fighting social discrimination through legal and constitutional ways
3. Developing Dalit women leadership

4. Sustainability of the social projects and building solidarity amongst the individuals and organizations

Buddhist practice and meditation are central to each activity. In Manuski's meditation hall, and at all the Indian meditation centers I have visited, one can sense the concentration and settledness in people's bodies and expressions, and in their respectful demeanor. Men come dressed in slacks and business shirts. Women wear bright saris, suggesting shared origins with the robes of monks and nuns. The meditation practices of TBM are straightforward and familiar: *anapanasati* or mindfulness of breathing and *metta bhavana*/cultivation of lovingkindness. In time these practices peacefully suffuse one's life.

Since Ambedkar himself was a Buddhist layman, and the first mass conversions took place among laypeople, it is not surprising that the new Buddhists have created a lay or lay-ordained movement. The organizational model of TBM is an order of *dhammacharis/dhammacharinis*— meaning followers of the dharma. Order members are meditation teachers, study leaders, and ministers. One can see them in this way: not quite priest, not quite lay.

TBM's network, like Indra's jeweled net, has many facets, each mutually reflecting the work of others. Meditation itself does not cure all ills. So, along with temples and storefront viharas, TBM has created retreat centers, hostels, adult education, atrocity and civil rights work, earthquake and tsunami relief, school programs, and more in Maharashtra, Uttar Pradesh, Gujurat, Tamil Nadu, Andhra Pradesh, and throughout India in diverse urban and local settings.

To Nagaloka

The backward classes have come to realize that after all education is the greatest material benefit for which they can fight. We may forego material benefits, we may forego material benefits of civilization, but we cannot forego our right and opportunities to reap the benefit of the highest education to the fullest extent.

— Dr. B. R. Ambedkar: *Writings and Speeche*s, Vol. 2

NAGPUR IS A SPRAWLING AND ragged city of two-and-a-half million. At the geographic center of India, Nagpur sits on the banks of the winding Nag River, Nag meaning serpent in Marathi, the local language. The city is low, flat, dusty, and ever expanding. Each time I visit, the suburbs reach a little farther into the surrounding countryside. Trucks roar and wheeze through the intersections of three national highways. Truck repair shops line the potholed roads north of the city. Nagpur is called the "Orange City," a fact I know only because there is a big orange sphere on a pedestal in the middle of town. Much of the year it is unpleasantly hot, though the winter, when I like to visit, is mild, even cool. Nagpur is ground zero for India's Dalit Buddhists.

In 1956 Ambedkar chose Nagpur as the place where he took public refuge in Buddhism and where he then turned around and offered the three Buddhist refuges to four hundred thousand Untouchables present at Nagpur's Deekshabhoomi or conversion ground. This was the birth of India's "new Buddhist" movement of ex-Untouchables. And it is here that Sangharakshita and TBM chose to create Nagaloka.

Nagaloka's fifteen-acre campus—the largest of TBM's Indian projects—is off the busy Kamptee Road, on the outskirts of the city, surrounded by marriage halls with their blaring sound systems. In the evening cool, from a distance one can see the forty-foot tall golden walking Buddha that smiles down on Nagaloka's students and local Buddhist families who come after work to relax, stroll through the grounds, and pay their respects to the Buddha.

The compound is spacious and green. Simple but stylish brick buildings, modeled on ancient Buddhist structures, are designed to be comfortably cool even in the heavy midday heat. Presently there are four residential buildings with facilities for students, guests and conferences, a classroom and library building, kitchen facilities, two elegant meditation halls, administrative offices, a rolling lawn and garden, and room for expansion in the future.

At Nagaloka's center is the Nagarjuna Training Institute, a residential engaged Buddhist training program for young women and men from all across India.

The objective of NTI's year-long program is to train these youth in meditation, basic Buddhism, and social thought and action so they can "return to their home regions and share their knowledge of the Dhamma and help create a society free of caste and discrimination."

During his 1992 visit to India, Urgen Sangharakshita, who had lived and studied in India between 1944 and 1964, proposed the idea of a large teaching facility outside Nagpur that could be a learning and activist center for Ambedkarite Buddhists all across India. The first building, the Buddha Surya Vihara, was completed in 1997. Classrooms, library, and residential facilities were completed in 2002, and the first one-year residential training program, the Nagarjuna Training Institute, was begun. All this has been made possible by the generosity of many friends in Taiwan, of Karuna Trust in the United Kingdom, and of dedicated donors elsewhere in Asia and the United States.

Over the last eleven years NTI has welcomed more than seven hundred young people from twenty-four states in India. These students are truly Ambedkar's children. They all come from impoverished rural backgrounds, gaining an education despite the high barriers of caste discrimination, poverty, and even violence. India is in the midst of an explosion of technology, education, productivity, and wealth. But even in the face of the nation's recent economic and technological development, Ambedkar's vision of an Indian future defined by "liberty, equality, and fraternity" depends on the up-lifting of the most oppressed.

The full-time residential program for seventy to a hundred youth includes meditation and chanting twice a day, classes, cultural activities, community work, and cultural activities. Babasaheb Ambedkar's writings and activities are at the heart of the school's vision and curriculum. As there are successive cohorts of graduates, one year's students help select candidates for the coming year's program. A wide network of Dhamma workers and supporters is taking shape, many of whom are actively teaching Buddhism and social action in their home villages or in other urban TBM projects.

The school explains its mission this way:

> The different Scheduled caste communities in India do not usually cooperate with each other, even after they have become Buddhists. At the Nagarjuna Institute they relate to each other just as Buddhists and not in terms of the caste they have come from. This in itself is an enormous contribution to a truly democratic society. The intensive practice for a year with other Buddhists from all over India means they cease to identify with the old untouchable caste but just as Buddhists.

I have been making annual visits to Nagaloka for the last five years—to teach, and learn, and spend time with the students. Usually I teach for a week or ten days, which is, admittedly, not a long time. But our studies have ranged widely: from engaged Buddhism in general to an examination of the Buddha's early social thinking, the present and historical situation of women in Buddhism, and the history of race relations in the United States. In each of these areas there are parallels and contrasts to be explored between the West and India. And in each case Dr. Ambedkar's precise and prophetic voice has something to teach us.

Nagaloka's students can also teach us—about oppression and violence, but, more powerfully, about education and self-respect, and the light of Buddha's wisdom and practice.

Nagaloka Lives

From my first visit to India I have made an effort to draw out the students' stories. We can learn from these compelling stories, and the students can learn from each other. One young man recounted:

> In my childhood I observed this caste system all the time. My grandmother had to take water from the village well. But when she put her bucket in, other community people saw that and would not take water until the well was purified by rituals. If someone asked you to their home for food, if you were Dalit, you had to wash your own plate. My father often used to do that. Once I was invited for dinner, but I refused to wash my plate. They asked why I wouldn't wash it. I said, if you invite me to eat with you, it is not right to force me to wash my own plate. In that case, I can give up your food and go. So I just left.

A woman of twenty said:

> I am from Orissa. Where I live there is still a very
> strong caste system. They don't allow Dalit children
> to get any kind of education. If a girl tries to get
> an education, their parents become afraid and get
> them married quickly. Neighborhood people will
> not allow the girls to learn as they wish to. We are
> here at Nagaloka now, but my family doesn't know
> we are learning Buddhism. When we go back to
> the village we will share with them what we have
> learned about the dharma. We came with the help
> of former students, and when we go back we will
> help find other students. I really believe that our
> training at Nagaloka will benefit our community.

In the winter of 2013, my wife Laurie and I went to India
and Nagaloka, as I have done for the last five winters.
We had sessions with students in the morning and afternoon. During the morning sessions we explored the history of race in the United States, from slavery, the Civil
War, and emancipation, through the civil rights movement of the 1950s and '60s, to the election of Barack
Obama. Actually, the students' first questions were
about Obama. How did a Black man, a kind of American
Untouchable, come to be elected president of the United
States?

Each afternoon we invited students to share their life
stories and how they came to Nagaloka and Buddhism.

Because their stories are colored by shame, students were initially reluctant to come forward. It can be intimidating for young people, or for anyone, to speak in front of others. (In the Buddha's list of the five "great fears," the fear of public speaking follows more obvious fears of death, illness, dementia, and loss of livelihood.) But after our first session students were lining up to tell their stories, and we knew we would not have enough time to hear them all.

The narratives here are stripped down. Each student had only twenty to thirty minutes, including translation from their own languages. Most of the on-the-spot translation was done by Utpala Chakma, a third-year Nagaloka student from Arunachal Pradesh.

The details of these students' lives are vivid, at times shocking. They are also inspiring. As we transcribed and edited their stories, certain common details stood out. All the students were from poor, rural backgrounds. The ten stories here provide a cross-section of Nagaloka's student body. These students come from six Indian states, some of them a thousand miles distant. They range in age from seventeen to twenty-two. All of them have experienced the double or triple oppression of caste, poverty, and gender discrimination. Each of these young people is fortunate to have at least one parent's support in getting an education and taking the bold step of leaving home for Nagaloka.

These are the lives of engaged Buddhists, new on the path but dedicated according to their faith and life experience.

Seema
Age 18, Rajasthan

WE ARE FIVE BROTHERS AND sisters.

My father used to own a grocery shop. He worked thirteen hours a day. Despite ill health, he continued to work. My mother had not studied at all, but still she encouraged her children to go to school.

My father had four brothers. One was in the military and the other three only had education up to the Fifth Standard. They all had their own houses except for my father. We had a very small place to live, only two rooms for my parents and five children. So my father went outside the village and built a small mud hut where we could live without paying rent. During the rainy season it was very difficult to sleep there because water was always dripping inside the house. Most of the time we had very little food at home. Often we had just one dish with sauce or chutney. We would wait for my father to return from work, but he could be late. Sometimes we couldn't wait any longer, so we just had the chutney.

My brother and sister were going to school. Most of my cousins were not taking education, and so they were quite jealous of us. They taunted my father: "You can't even make a good house to live in, how will you support your children's studies?" But my father was strong in heart. He was determined that his children would study, take good jobs, and make a good living in the future.

I studied through Class Eight in the village. After that I had to go outside the village until I completed the Twelfth Standard. My elder brother studied, like me, up to Eighth Standard in the village, then attended school in another town. He got his BA and is working as a teacher. My younger brother studied up to the Tenth Standard in my village. He moved to my uncle's house, did his further studies, and got a job in the IT sector.

Two of my uncles were not of good nature. Because of jealousy, they constantly pushed my brother and sisters to get married. Their children had no education but my brother and sister were on the track of studies. They picked fights with my father and sometimes they would even try to choke him.

Now I am just studying at home and at Nagaloka. I am in my first year of a course towards a BA at a college in Rajasthan. All my brothers are working. My sister was not interested in school; she only went up to the Tenth. So she was given in marriage.

My parents say we are a Hindu family, but they never perform any Hindu rites and rituals. Most of my other relatives were against my coming here to Nagaloka. But my father and my mother supported me. They felt, if our daughter does this, others may be inspired. Also, my cousin A. is here. My elder brother sent him to Nagaloka so he could study and stand on his own feet. I am the first girl from my village to travel so far from home and to study Buddhism. I knew very little about Buddhism as a religion, but I heard that in Buddhism there is no God.

Girls are being tortured and oppressed in Rajasthan. I would love to teach the girls in my village and inspire them to go for higher education.

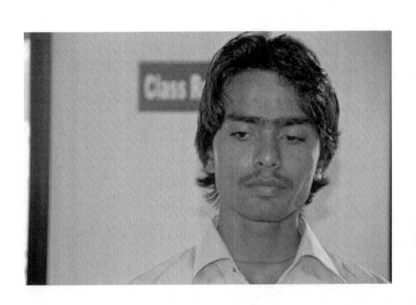

Pradip
Age 18, Rajasthan

ORIGINALLY I CAME FROM A very poor area. My family has had to struggle to have a normal life, a good life. My father used to work in government, now he is a social worker. My grandfather was a follower of the poet Kabir. When he started reading Kabir, he found that Kabir was very far from all the gods and goddesses in Hinduism. So my father never believed in Hinduism. In the city he found Dr. Ambedkar's books and started reading about Buddhism. That is how he became Buddhist. My mother finished the Tenth Standard in school. She takes care of our home and helps my father with his social work sometimes.

In 1998 my father stood for office in the local election, but he had to withdraw because of untouchability and other social problems. It is difficult if you come from a Scheduled Caste background. Around the time of that election we had some economic status, but after some years it started deteriorating.

Because he was focused on the economic problems at home, my father was not able to give proper attention to the children. But still he tried to create a good environment for three of the sons at home, and to educate them well. My eldest brother works at a bank. My second brother is not working. And I am the third. I started at the government school, then was admitted to private school, pursuing education in the Hindi medium.

I want to talk about some events that inspired me to come to Nagaloka. In my village the high-caste people have the power. In India we have Holi, a Hindu festival. [This is the festival of colors, which marks the beginning of Spring season.] During this festival high-caste people from my village broke into the home of a young woman who was six or seven months pregnant. She was alone at the time. They raped her and pulled her out of the house, leaving not even a single piece of cloth on her body. Few people in the village took her side.

People from my family and other village people of the same caste wanted justice for this lady. The case was brought to the village court. But because the perpetrators were both wealthy and high caste, even this committee of village chiefs supported the people who did the crime, not the woman.

After this incident there was another incident with my uncle's daughter. My cousin was getting married in a Buddhist ceremony. The high-caste people said there could be no marriage procession. They threatened that if the procession came into the village, it would not come out again. My father, being involved in social work, knew what could happen, so beforehand he made arrangements for police protection. Still the high-caste people were stubborn and tried to block the procession. But my relatives and other village people kept guns for their protection, even though they did not have proper licenses. So the marriage ceremony was successful, and the high-caste people were upset and held a grudge.

Conditions in our village continue to be the same. Scheduled Caste women are not allowed to draw water from the well. The roads in front of the homes of SC people are not proper roads, just muddy tracks. SC children are not allowed to pursue a proper education in the local schools where caste students go.

Again, this is a village where high-caste Hindu people have power and they suppress the scheduled castes. The high-caste people lend money to SC farmers. If the scheduled-caste people are not able to repay these loans, the lenders take their land. They still hold onto those lands.

Rajasthan is said to have been an empire of kings and queens, equal in war as well as in other strategies for saving the empire. This equality is deteriorating day by day. People have forgotten the importance of women in Rajasthan. I think this is something they should know and think about.

Looking at the condition of women, Rajasthan is a bit like the neighboring state of Haryana. In Haryana they have brutal rituals, killing girl children. I have often thought about this—why is India a male-dominant country? Girls have the ability to do everything. In India a woman can do manual labor, and she can even rise to become the president.

I want to help people see that killing infant girls is wrong. I want to help people understand that there is no difference between a girl and a boy.

Pradip is now in the Twelfth Standard at school. After school he hopes to become an air force officer.

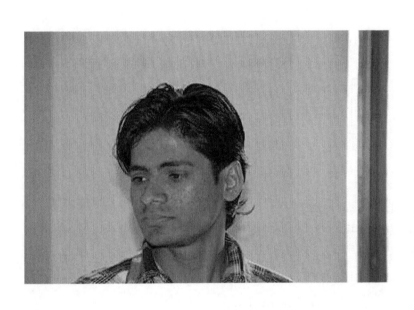

Anand
Age 19, Rajasthan

I come from Rajasthan. I want to share something about my life. When I was five my father left and had a second marriage. My father often worked in Katmandu, Nepal. He liked another woman there and got married without our knowledge. I used to think that if ever I met my father, either he would die or I would. But now, understanding Buddhism, I would want to forgive him.

My mother lived with us at home, and the three of us, brothers and sisters, had very little money for our education. She took us to Haryana. There were three rooms in my uncle's house there, so he gave us one of the rooms to live in. I studied there for three years in a private school.

My grandfather took responsibility for the three of us, asking my maternal uncle to keep us with him and take care of our further education and marriage. At that time we were living in a very big family in a village—my uncles, my mother, my aunts, two brothers, and two married sisters, all staying in one big house with my grandfather and grandmother.

All three of my uncles were continuously drinking. The joint family did not work, so they broke into separate units, and we went with our grandfather. From the Second Standard, I did my education in the village. But after several years, our grandfather was continuously harassing us, telling us to find work, make our own money, and leave his house. I was nine years old.

My mother was working as a day laborer. Doing day labor she was supporting me to continue my education. In 2007, both of my sisters got married. After Class Nine I studied outside the village.

I had not seen my father, but I could recognize him from photographs. When one of my aunts got married, my father came to the wedding. When he arrived, I saw him, but he did not recognize me. Others had to tell him, "This is your son." But he did not attend my sisters' weddings. I was not feeling good about that. So I called and spoke to him.

One of my sisters had a baby boy. There was a tradition that whenever a male child is born, family members will give some gifts to the boy. My mother went to visit her daughter. Then I heard that my uncles were trying to kill my mother, so we quickly came back to their house. By the time we got there many things had taken place. The neighbors said that my uncles were trying to kill my mother with an axe. Somehow she was able to resist that. She had locked herself inside a room and was safe for now.

When I asked her, my mother said, "I don't know what happened, but my brother came home drunk and started to beat me. When I saw the axe in his hand, I locked myself in a room. I sent my mother to my other maternal uncle's house so she would be safe.

Several months later my mother became very ill. After completing the Twelfth Standard, I began working in computers and videography. Whatever money I earned I used to buy medicines for my mother. Once I had a quarrel with my colleagues at the computer job. After the quarrel my mom told me to leave that job. Then I was doing just the video work. Once, when there was a lot of work, I was not allowed to sleep for seven days straight. My mom found out about that and told me to quit that job too.

The medicines I bought were helping to keep my mom alive, but when I was not working, I could not buy medicine. When the medicine stopped, she died. I felt then that this life is full of care and sadness. What should I do? Is there any reason to be alive in this world? But my sisters and cousins helped me take care of my life.

A relative from Rajhastan, a Nagaloka alumnus, was working in Delhi, and he encouraged me to come here. I was inspired by Dr. Ambedkar's book, *The Buddha and His Dharma.* I wanted to know more about it. In our village, no one really knows about the Buddha and Babasaheb Ambedkar, but whenever there is a marriage ceremony, we can see two photos on the altar, one of the Buddha and one of Dr. Ambedkar.

After graduation from Nagaloka, Anand wants resume his course of study. He is planning to study Chinese. After that he would like to travel and show Buddhist sites to people.

Sangita
Age 20, Chattisghar

❦

I WAS BORN IN A tribal family; my parents do agricultural work. Though my parents were uneducated, they intended for me to get an education. In my village there were no schools, no hospitals, and no electricity. In my father's childhood, one village schoolmaster used to come to teach the small children, but my father didn't pay any attention and remained uneducated. That same teacher was there when I was born, and I studied with her for my first few years of school.

In my village I studied up to primary level. Then the Naxalites [a Maoist paramilitary group which dominates her region] opened their own school. I continued my studies there. There was a student who had graduated from Nagaloka, from the Eighth Class there, and he contacted me. I've always had a feeling that I would go far from my village to study. I had never heard of Babasaheb Ambedkar or Buddhism, but when I heard about this opportunity to study, I packed up my bags before I'd even talked with my parents. But my parents supported me to go. When I came to Nagaloka, I was the first woman who has studied beyond the Twelfth Standard from my village.

Actually here is what happened in my village: my parents continuously supported my education, but the Naxalites discouraged parents from sending their children for higher education. This is a very difficult local situation. The Naxalites discourage education because they worry that educated young people are likely to join the police force, whom they see as their enemy. Some villagers try to go to school, if there is police protection. There are nursery schools in her village, but few students go there, because the Naxalites threaten them. Often young people are taken by the Naxalites into the forest and trained to use guns.

My elder brother studied in a college in a city far from home. Some of the villagers informed the Naxalites that he was studying to become a policeman.

When my brother came home after taking his exams, one day he was out in a field. Naxalites came and tied up his hands and feet, wrapped him up in a cloth, and carried him away. When my father came home, the family went to search for him. The Naxalites had taken him to another village and were keeping him prisoner in the forest. But the villagers who knew where he was were afraid to say anything. After my family promised that they would not reveal who had given them the information, one family finally told them where he had been taken. They searched the whole night, but they didn't find him. Finally they went to the Naxalites to ask them where he was. They said, "Your son is very sick. We haven't done anything to him, he will be fine." My father, perhaps, gave some money to the Naxalites, and that's why they freed him. In the morning they brought my brother, and he had been beaten very badly. They had told him, "Next time, don't go anywhere, don't go for studies, just stay in your village." The Naxalites threatened the villagers, saying, "We can do the same thing to you if you complain about this."

My brother felt, "If I go for further studies, I will be killed, but if I stay here, I will also be killed. So it will be a good thing for me to go for a job as a policeman. I may be killed, but I will be helping my nation, and that's my first priority." He worked as a policeman for five years, got married, and had two children. Then the Naxalites set a trap for him. They told him that there was emergency, and he ran to help. Other police came, and he went with them in their jeep. Then the Naxalites blew up the jeep. My brother dragged himself out of the jeep and then he was shot.

My sister-in-law was offered her husband's job, but she turned it down. Instead she became the village headperson. She stays at the police station, and has police protection for her activities in the village. The Naxalites don't know that she is serving this role. But the village is divided into two groups—one group supports the Naxalites, and the other group supports the government and are somewhat protected by the government.

Sangita's brother wanted her to become a policeman, but she will not do that. She wants to do something good for her community, and good for humanity. Sangita plans to stay at Nagaloka for three years.

Bosu
Age 22, Arunachal Pradesh

My name is Bosu. I come from Arunachal Pradesh, from the Chakma people. Now I'm going to talk about my life. My family came to India in exile from Bangladesh before I was born.

When I was about six or seven years old, I was a very naughty boy. I used to teach my friends how to annoy people and make people angry. I was very skilled at this and very naughty. Several times I was beaten by my mother.

In 1998, when I was about nine years old, my mother died in childbirth because she could not get proper medical care. After that my father was left with the burden of our family. My grandmother and grandfather looked after me and my younger sister while my father worked very hard at agriculture.

My studies continued, and after completing Class Eight, my intention was to take higher education. I was able to study up to Standards Eleven and Twelve. But during this time I had a dangerous disease. The doctors said I suffered from irritable bowel syndrome, IBS. After trying many medicines, all in vain, there was no benefit. I was considered hopeless. I thought I was going to die.

All of my relatives were very worried. They wanted to support me to destroy this disease. Now I am doing a treatment. My father encouraged me. He said: "Don't worry, it will take time. You will be a completely healthy person."

Some people in my home area claim they are Buddhist, but they don't really know much about Buddhism. When I was in Class Six, a monk came from Bangladesh to meet us and see our situation. That bhikkhu was the disciple of Ven. Bana Bhante, the late spiritual leader of the Chakma people in the Chittagong Hill Tracts of Bangladesh. Because of him the Chakma people in Bangladesh and India are developing.

Students who had been to Nagaloka told me about the school, but I was not listening at first. Last year when I was staying in his village I met M., a former student. He visited our home and asked me what I was doing at the time. I was in Class Twelve and I wanted to go to college. Even though we were very poor, I was trying to figure out what to do. M. said I could go to Nagaloka if I wanted to. So I did.

Bosu says: "After graduation, I will support my community in society, according to my power, according to my mental ability. I will serve. But I don't know how yet. After graduation, I'll think about that."

Vanita
Age 18, Arunachal Pradesh

I'M GOING TO TELL MY life story for the first time, in front of all of you. I was sickly when I was born so I was not able to help my parents, who were farmers. Even though my parents are Hindu, they know about Babasaheb Ambedkar. My father drinks continuously and beats my mother. We are a total of five children in the village. Two of my sisters are already married. One of my sisters is doing her studies, and one sister is working with my parents. I also have an elder brother who used to work driving a tractor. Whatever money he got, he used to buy some cooking oil for the house.

We have very difficult conditions at home. We only have one real meal per day. In the evening we only have dry chapatis. Our relatives cannot help us. My younger sister is very helpful and supportive to me, though she is not taking education. She works in the fields, and whatever money she gets goes to support my parents and me. She buys food for the family each day. But then the next day they have no food. Nothing stored up.

Until Class Eight I studied in the village school, which was ten kilometers from my home. My mother told me that I didn't need to continue after Class Eight. I should come and help in the fields. Though my father was a drunkard, he still supported me to continue my studies. Through Class Twelve I stayed at home and went to school by bus. I have never gone far from my village. My village is very rural, no electricity, no phones. I've hardly gone out of my house, so I don't really know what other problems people are facing there.

Three senior Nagaloka students came to my village and talked to my father and mother about allowing me to come to Nagaloka. It was very difficult to convince them. Also it was hard to communicate. My parents only spoke Telugu, not Hindi or Marathi. Because of my illness, my father was reluctant to give me permission. They were afraid something might happen when I was far from home. But I was very enthusiastic about coming to Nagaloka and continuing my studies. Because the Nagaloka students were willing to travel with me, my parents were willing to let me go.

I am happy that I came to Nagaloka, so far from my home. I don't really want to go back home, because it's very difficult in my village. My parents have never called me, even once, in these six months, so I've been very sad about that.

When I was at school, many of the students were unfriendly to me, but at Nagaloka all the students are my good friends. I am very happy about this. The most important thing is that I've never spoken up in front of anyone. At Nagaloka I have a great opportunity to express myself in front of all the people.

Vanita has not finished her Twelfth Standard, so she'll complete that after going home. After graduation, she hopes to help the people in her village.

Raj
Bihar

FIRST I WILL SAY SOMETHING about my ancestors. For many years we lived in a small village where there were only three families. Nearby there was a jungle and no other people. Time passed, generation followed generation, and now there are twenty-four families.

My grandfather used to work in the Jharia coal fields. He was a devotee of the Hindu god Hanuman, and he used to sing *bhajans* celebrating Hanuman. My father would go with him and watch him work in the coalfields.

One day a family friend brought my grandfather home drunk. My father stayed in the coalfield and somehow he had an attack of paralysis on one side of his body.

My father's family was very poor. No proper clothes, no good food. But my father was in school. My grandmother supported his studies, but my grandfather was not happy about this, so he collected all my father's books and papers and burned them.

In 1977 my father was the first person in his whole village to complete the matriculation exam. There was a huge quarrel because a scheduled-caste boy had passed, ahead of the upper-caste boys. This was not supposed to happen.

My father got married, and their first two children died at birth. My elder brother also died, at the age of seventeen. It was believed that in the area where the school was located most of the village women were witches. Those boys who were good at school fell prey to a witch. This is said to have happened to my brother.

After that my four sisters were born, and then they had two boys, so we were the youngest. My first sister was helping my parents with work. Two sisters were going to school, one was still very young. My elder sister used to graze the cows and animals. Some of the teachers saw her and they urged her to go to school. At first she thought, it's useless to study. Later on she changed her mind, and decided she should also learn to read and write. She was good at studies, so she went to the Fifth Standard, and continued from there.

It happened that all my sisters and brothers were in the same school. The villagers didn't approve of these girls taking higher education. They taunted my sisters as they walked to school. One year my sisters got first degrees on the final exam for their respective classes.

On the prize distribution day, they all got awards. Some people thought these prizes might be valuable, so that night a thief came to our house and stole their prizes and jewelry. Later, out in a big field, they found all the prizes torn apart. Just books and pens and pencils left behind. The thieves kept the jewelry.

Our school was run by a big institution with many branches. Due to some problem in their management, and corruption maybe, the schools were all closed in 2005, and nearly a thousand students had to stop their studies.

We had a sponsor in America supporting our studies. He gave us money for books and school materials. By then, my father had become a drunkard. Whatever we could earn by working in the fields was used for food, household expenses and maintenance.

I was living at home, not at a hostel. I didn't have any money at all. My grandmother used to give me two rupees each day. For two rupees I could buy eight biscuits. That was all the food I had. In the rainy season, our clothes would get drenched in the rain. The school was very strict about the rules. We had to wear our uniforms properly, and if we were not neatly dressed we were punished for it. These were difficult conditions. At last, out of sympathy, they gave me some breakfast at nine in the morning. I went all day on that one meal.

Our American sponsor continued to support all of us. So far I have completed the Twelfth Standard. My first and second sister have almost graduated. My third sister is in her last year, and the fourth is in intermediate school.

All of them are married and working, too. My first sister is a teacher for girls from poor areas. Because these girls' parents won't allow them to go to the government school, they come to my sister's house to study.

Some former students told me about Nagaloka. I thought I would come and see if the environment seemed useful to me. I thought that I might benefit from being here, so I decided to stay for the eight-month program. Then I will go back home.

Aruna
Age 17, Karnatika

BEFORE NOW I HAVEN'T SHARED my life history in front of so many people. But I have shared it with some of my close friends and some of our seniors. So today I'm going to speak about how I faced many problems in my home and society.

I feel that my life is full of sadness. We are three sisters in my family. I don't have any brothers of my own, but I have some cousins. My younger sister and I stayed at home for a long time. Our middle sister, M., who is present here at Nagaloka, lived at our grandmother's from childhood through the Tenth Class.

I didn't face much caste discrimination in the village but there were other problems in my family. From childhood I studied in my village through the Third Standard, and then I went to my grandmother's home for a time. After returning from my grandmother's, I felt very lonely in my home village because I had left most of my friends. My mother is a tailor and my father is a carpenter. Whatever money my mother earned from tailoring was wasted by my father. My father is a drunkard, so he and his friends regularly spent the money that was earned by my mom.

My dad took some education, but still he was not aware of how to lead a proper family life, how to take care of his family. Society was like that. Even if somebody is going on the right path, society and friends will sometimes pull you down. My father was leading a life like that. I used to talk with him about this matter, that you should follow the right path and lead a good life; and he would always say—yes, yes. But afterwards he would turn to drinking again.

But my mom was completely different. She was always encouraging us to take good education and helping us in our studies. Whatever I've done in my life, whatever study and education, the credit goes to my mom.

Until the Fifth Standard I used to go to walk to school, but after Fifth I went by bicycle. Most of my uncles and aunts were jealous about my taking higher education. In my school days much of the time I was worrying about my family. I was worried that my father was beating my mom after drinking or that she had other difficulties. I shared these feelings with my mom, and she advised me to concentrate on my studies. She suggested that I read more and more, and make sure to get a good education. "Don't worry about how your father treats me, I will bear it silently."

During my higher secondary exams, my mother expected me to take distinctions, but after I did get first class, many of my uncles urged my parents to have me married and not to take any higher college education. But my mom stayed firm. She helped me apply for college.

When I began college, at that time I could not find friends so I felt very lonely. When exams came, I had to walk five kilometers to school, because though there were buses, the people on the buses didn't have good character. Whatever problems I had I shared with my mom, and she used to encourage me in all kinds of situations. I think my mom is my best friend.

At some time during my college days, some of my uncles came to arrange my marriage. In south India the custom is for marriage to be arranged between maternal uncles and nieces. Some other relations came for marriage from Bangalore. They were a rich family, working in banks, very rich. My mother refused to give her permission for the marriage, but her brothers tried to force her to make me marry. By then I was taking spoken English classes. Some of my friends are here; we four used to go together for English classes. One day, while I was at English class, my uncles came and told me, "If you don't agree to marry we'll kidnap you at the bus stand." They communicated this matter to their relatives, who said, "If anything happens to her, there is a police station nearby; we will go to the police."

This was reported to my mother, and she suggested that I should be very alert. So I got in contact with an ex-Nagaloka student from Karnatika, and she came with three other students to help with security. I feel that whatever problems I have I share with my friends here. I'm very grateful to my friends.

Aruna's goal is to find a position in the Indian Administrative Service or be a social worker.

Suman
Age 22, Uttar Pradesh

I WOULD LIKE TO SHARE my experience, some of the incidents that took place in my life. When I was born my parents loved me very much. They had a big attachment to me, and they were very supportive of my education. They knew a little about Buddhism. But I did not know my older brothers and sisters, because they were not living at home.

I had one elder sister; she was given away in marriage. After two years of marriage she died. One of my elder brothers was sent out from my village to study. When I was five years old I started at one of the primary schools. My parents decided to send me away from home to live with my brothers so I could continue with school studies. When I went there, my father explained to me: "This is your brother, this is your brother." And at that time I found out that these were my family members. I was not sure that I would be able to manage, because I had never spent any time with them.

I stayed with them for four years. There were two brothers studying. One brother failed the Tenth Standard three times, so he went back to my home, and I came with him. Again we took admission in the village school. We had to walk for seven kilometers to school.

Another brother was studying outside the village. He also failed the Tenth Class, and he also came back to our home. My dad was very worried and very sad about this.

It was being discussed that I should also stop, but the decision was made that I must carry on with my studies. My brothers were not happy about this decision. They used to beat me. "Why are you going to study? You will not do anything good." My father was a doctor—not a practicing doctor, but a village doctor—and he went out for the whole day. At home, in his absence, my brothers used to beat me.

Only my father supported me. He told the brothers, "If you continue beating her, I will leave home and take her with me." Once again they beat me so much. They held my neck and tried to choke me. My mother came in and separated them.

My brothers are still at home. One is working in agriculture and the other is a mechanic. But I haven't been home for two years. Whenever I call home, my father answers the phone, not my brothers.

After the Eighth Standard a teacher tried to force me not to take science, but I chose to continue. One day the science teacher came for the class, and he said, "I don't want you in my class. Either I will stay here or you will stay here." This was on account of caste. But because one of my friends was encouraging me, I stood on my two feet. No one could make me leave that class. The teacher did come to class that day, but with my friends' help I stood strong and was able to stay. The principal was very supportive. That teacher left and the principal said they would get another teacher.

At last, after the exams, I passed into the Second Division, that is Tenth Standard. The principal told me, "If you are going to take science in English, it will be very difficult for you, because you don't have the English background." So while taking admission for Class Eleven I chose to study in English, but at first they didn't allow me because my maths were not that good. It was a school with students from various caste backgrounds, but still there was caste discrimination.

Taking the subjects in English, I faced a lot of problems. There was no real support for my education from most of the teachers. But one teacher used to tutor me. In 2007 I passed Class Twelve, but because I got low marks in one subject I decided to take the Twelfth for a second time. After that I went to college and received a BA in history and English.

There are many students at Nagaloka from UP. They brought their friends to visit and went to the ceremonies here. When they returned from Nagaloka they told me about it. My father brought me here.

Harshita
Age 18, Uttar Pradesh

JAI BHIM... I COME FROM Uttar Pradesh, UP, and we are a family of five brothers and sisters. When I was five years old I was admitted to school. There was no school in my village, so I had to travel two kilometers to school. My father didn't follow Hinduism, but others in the village were Hindu. Since I came to Nagaloka, I am trying to be a Buddhist.

My parents have some education so they encouraged me to go to school. I used to be tortured by the other school children there. They would say, "Why do you come to our town site to study? Don't you have schools in your village?" After some years my family moved nearer the school, so my sisters and brothers are able to study there. But still there is no school in the village where I grew up, and it is difficult for girls to study.

After graduation from school, the time for marriage was fast approaching. I wanted a well-educated husband. When my parents looked for an educated husband for me, the other parents demand a high dowry. In villages the old people often think that if the girls are educated then the dowry price will rise. So it's better not to teach girls much; just some basic knowledge like how to write their name and how to add two plus two.

Some former students from my village told me about Nagaloka. The Nagaloka training is helping women like me find confidence. I have dreams for my village, to do something good for the people there. When I told people in college that I was going to Nagaloka for a one-year training in Buddhism, my teacher, who was a Brahmin, was not happy about it. But he said one thing: if you learn something from that religion, come and teach me. So I remember this teacher's words. I hope to go back and teach him.

Now I am in my second year towards a BA. I have to travel twenty-five kilometers to college. Because I am studying so far from home, people in my village say that my parents have lost control of me. While I am here at Nagaloka some there say, "We don't know, maybe she's not going to come back."

The place I come from is a very male-dominated place. Every task needs a man's permission. If there is no male involvement, the task won't be done. So there is discrimination against women and caste discrimination in my region. Even the Brahmins in our village don't treat women properly.

In my neighborhood, there was a Brahmin family. Their daughter was married for just a couple of months when her husband died very suddenly. In the Brahmin caste, if you become a widow you cannot remarry. So, even though she was still young she couldn't remarry. She was nowhere.

This woman lived in a hut made of dried grass. She was pregnant when her husband died, and she gave birth to a boy. Even then she was not allowed a share of her husband's property. Nothing from her in-laws' side and no support from her parents. She was treated very badly by all of her relatives. Fortunately she got a job at a primary school, making lunch for the school children. Still, she wasn't given any importance, and people in the village want her to leave.

Harshita says: "When I was a child I aspired to become a police officer. But as I am short....(laughter)...now I want to complete my college course after this training. I'd like to get a bachelor's degree in education and become a teacher."

Three Refuges —
Liberty, Equality,
Fraternity

THE LIVES ABOVE PAINT PICTURES of young people reinventing themselves. As they absorb the Buddha's practices and Ambedkar's social thought, the chains of caste begin to fall away. As they discover self-respect, a new and practical vision comes into focus. In an All-India Radio broadcast two years before his conversion, Dr. Ambedkar said:

> Positively, my social philosophy may be said to be enshrined in three words: liberty, equality and fraternity. Let no one, however, say that I have borrowed my philosophy from the French Revolution. I have not. My philosophy has its roots in religion and not in political science. I have derived them from the teachings of my master, the Buddha.

After Ambedkar's 1956 conversion he taught the Buddha's traditional Three Refuges—Buddha, Dharma,

Sangha. Taking Refuge in these Three Treasures is the universal expression of commitment to the Buddha's Way. One morning as I lay in bed at TBM's Kondhanpur retreat center, I realized that these two ideals merge into one. At the moment it seemed like an original insight. But when I mentioned it to Lokamitra he laughed, saying this had been a central point of discussions about Ambedkarite Buddhism in the early 1980s.

Liberty means being Buddha. It is the quality of actualized liberation, embodied by the Buddha. It implies the ability to have control over one's actions. As Dr. Ambedkar writes: "...liberty means the destruction of the dominion which one man holds over another..."

The north Indian society that Shakyamuni Buddha was born into so many years ago was not long on liberty. Lives were defined and controlled according to caste, gender, occupation, tribe, and so on. When the Buddha created his Sangha, liberty was its pivot and goal.

Our understanding of liberty is the entwining of individual freedom and social responsibility. In the realization of enlightened life, liberty is a practice, something that must be aspired to and worked at. It is not a static quality.

Equality is dharma, or something like universal law, in the sense that we see all beings as equal. In my own Mahayana Zen Buddhist tradition the eighteenth-century Master Hakuin's "Song of Meditation" says: "From the beginning all beings are Buddha." Each and every sentient being is precious and equal. All people are chosen—not just those of a particular religion, caste, gender, or nation. Dr. Ambedkar writes:

> Equality may be a fiction but nonetheless one must accept it as the governing principle...the question is, shall we treat them as unequal because they are unequal?... it can be urged that if it is good for the social body to get the most out of its members, it can get most out of them only by making them equal as far as possible at the very start of the race.
> — Dr. Ambedkar: *Annihilation of Caste*, 1936

Ambedkar understood that each person has strengths and weaknesses, skills and shortcomings. In this respect we are unique beings, unequal, and individual. But taken together, liberty and equality encourage us to be completely ourselves, as large and open as possible, respecting and valuing each other as precious.

Fraternity is the cutting edge of Ambedkar's Buddhism and India's new Buddhist movement. Fraternity is sangha, the community of practitioners, and the wider community of all beings (hence, linked to equality). In the Buddha's time there was a "fourfold sangha"—monks, nuns, laymen, laywomen. In many places, modern Asian Buddhism has reduced this to the onefold sangha—just monks. This was not Ambedkar's idea of Buddhism. Nor is a singular male monastic model likely to be the way forward for Buddhism in today's world.

Fraternity is a challenge for the Dalit community. The social realities of India draw clear lines between all the religions—Hindu, Muslim, Sikh, Christian, and Buddhist; between caste and non-caste peoples, even among the various groups who see themselves as Buddhist. The many Dalit groups themselves are often caught within a system of "graded inequality," where each Dalit group competes with another for the tiniest privileges of social position, economic opportunity, and political power. Fraternity, in Ambedkar's terms, is a kind of binding energy, according to a person's or a group's ability to set aside difference and privilege...and only connect.

There is much in this new Indian Buddhism that we share in the West. On both sides we look to the dharma in response to the Buddha's central message: *I teach about suffering and the end of suffering.* Often alienated from the religious traditions we were born to, many of us in the West come to Buddhism to meet our suffering and society's suffering directly. For Dalits, whose material circumstances may be so different from ours, the motivation is the same: to learn about suffering and to reach its end, in each person's life and in society.

The unity of dharma practice and our work in society is compassion in action. In the West and in India,

Buddhist centers and groups are involved in feeding the poor, chaplaincy, working in prisons and jails, organizing against discrimination and against war. We see this as a responsibility that flows from the bodhisattva vow to save all beings. From the start, Dr. Ambedkar's vision of Buddhism incorporated a vision of society and social liberation, far beyond the self-involved or nihilistic caricature that some people project on Buddhism. With Ambedkar as a teacher, it is natural that an Indian Buddhism movement, rooted in the lives and practice of the most oppressed, would see the oneness of personal development and social transformation.

Ambedkarite Buddhists hunger for the teachings and for contact with the wider world. Very few teachers or practitioners from the Buddhist world—Asian and Western—go to India to support TBM and other Ambedkarite groups. It is not that the Dalits need Buddhist "missionaries." Native Indian teachers are well trained in the Buddha's teachings. But they need our help, our resources, and they need to be seen and valued in the world. As the dharma takes root in slums and in the poorest villages across India and in places like Nagaloka and other refuges, we can learn, be inspired, and rededicate ourselves to liberation for all beings, irrespective of class, caste, gender, and tribe.

In the poor neighborhoods of Mumbai, Nagpur, Pune, and other cities scattered across the sprawling Indian subcontinent, running water is often a spigot down the block. Toilets might be a quiet corner behind a building, an abandoned lot, or a communal structure with three or four filthy stalls and no plumbing. Electricity comes by way of a makeshift cable spliced into the mainline. But life is everywhere tenacious. Joy springs up in unlikely places.

Along with storefront Hindu shrines and mosques, in these Indian cities it is common to come across a Buddhist *vihara*. A plastic tarp or corrugated roof covers an open square surrounded by shops and shanties. A golden Buddha adorned with fresh flowers sits beside a garlanded image of Babasaheb Ambedkar, both within a small wooden enclosure. Worn carpets are rolled out; men sit on one side, women on the other. City sounds rise within the silence of meditation—children's shouts, buzzing cycles and rickshaws, barking dogs, the crack of a cricket bat, a street vendor's cry. The peace of friends sitting together in meditation includes all of this and goes beyond it.

Here and everywhere, enlightenment is unfolding in the simple, common human activity of sitting down. The ancient Buddhas are here with us in the cool glow of evening. Dr. Ambedkar is here, too. In just this moment—which cannot be captured or defiled—freedom is at hand.

ACKNOWLEDGMENTS

THANKS TO MY DHARMA SISTERS and brothers in India: Dhammachari Lokamitra, Mangesh Dahiwale, Dhammachari Vivekaratna, Dhammachari Nagamitra, Dhammachari Maitreyanth, Utpala Chakma, Anjalee Askhobhya, Aspi Mistry, and to all the students and teachers at Nagaloka. In the U.S. thanks to Kate Giplin for her sharp editorial eye. I am grateful for my teachers and dharma friends: Dhammachari Viradhamma, Joanna Macy, Sulak Sivaraksa, David Loy, Sojun Weitsman Roshi, Linda Hess, and—always—Laurie Senauke.

- *The Buddha and His Dharma*, B. R. Ambedkar: Re-published for free distribution by The Corporate Body of the Buddha Educational Foundation, Taiwan <www.budaedu.org/en/book/II-02main.php3>
- *The Essential Writings of B. R. Ambedkar*, V Rodrigues (ed), Delhi: Oxford University Press, 2002.
- *Dr. Ambedkar and Untouchability*, Christophe Jaffrelot, Delhi: Paul's Press, 2005.
- *Ambedkar: Towards an Enlightened India*, Gail Omvedt, New Delhi: Penguin/Viking, 2004.
- *Dr. Babasaheb Ambedkar: The Untold Truth*, film, directed by Jabbar Patel, Mumbai: 2008.
- *Jai Bhim—Dispatches from a Peaceful Revolution*, Terry Pilchik (Nagabodhi), Glasgow: Windhorse, 2004.
- *Ambedkar and Buddhism*, Sangharakshita, Glasgow: Windhorse, 1986.
- *The Bodhisattva's Embrace: Dispatches from Engaged Buddhism's Front Lines*, Hozan Alan Senauke, Berkeley: Clear View Press, 2010.
- *From Untouchable to Dalit: Essays on the Ambedkar Movement*, Eleanor Zelliot, New Delhi: Manohar, 1996.

- *Behind the Beautiful Forevers: Life, Death, and Hope in a Mumbai Undercity,* Katherine Boo, New York: Random House, 2012.
- *Maximum City: Bombay Lost and Found,* Suketu Mehta, New York: Vintage, 2004.

Links:
www.TBM.org
www.clearviewproject.org
www.nagaloka.org
www.manuski.org
www.navayan.com
www.dharmajiva.org

Nagaloka: Kamptee Road, Near Akashwani Tower Bhilgaon, Nagpur, 441002 INDIA

HOZAN ALAN SENAUKE IS A Soto Zen Buddhist priest in the tradition of Shunryu Suzuki Roshi. He serves as vice-abbot of Berkeley Zen Center, where he has lived with his wife Laurie and his children for nearly thirty years. Hozan is founder of the Clear View Project, developing Buddhist-based resources for relief and social change in Burma and India. For years he was executive director of Buddhist Peace Fellowship and remains active in BPF as Senior Advisor. Alan is also on the International Network of Engaged Buddhists' Advisory Council. In another realm, Alan has been a close student and active performer of American traditional music for more than fifty years.

A person whose mind is not free, though he is not in chains, is a slave. One whose mind is not free, though he is not in jail, is a prisoner. One whose mind is not free, though he is alive, is dead. Freedom of mind is the proof of one's existence.

— Dr. B. R. Ambedkar: *What Path to Salvation?*, 1936

Made in the USA
San Bernardino, CA
04 August 2016